Assessment of Attachment-Related Pathology Surrounding Divorce

C.A. Childress, Psy.D.

Oaksong Press

Copyright © 2017 C.A. Childress

All rights reserved.

ISBN: 978-0-9961145-7-8

CONTENTS

Attachment-Related Family Pathology 1

    Healthy Child Development 1

    The "Custody Prize" 4

    Attachment Conflict 5

    Pathogenic Parenting 8

    Triangulation 9

Assessing for Pathogenic Parenting 13

    Assessing the Targeted Parent 13

    Assessing the Allied Parent 15

    The Narcissistic-Borderline Parent 16

    Session Protocol 18

    Stimulus Control and Behavior Chain Assessment 19

    Treatment-Focused Assessment Reports 21

Appendix 1: Parenting Practices Rating Scale 23

Appendix 2: Diagnostic Checklist for Pathogenic Parenting 27

Appendix 3: Example Reports 31

Attachment-Related Family Pathology

In family conflicts surrounding divorce, the issue that is often presenting to the Court is to determine the child custody and visitation schedule for the post-divorce family. When the custody and visitation schedule cannot be mutually agreed to by the parents, the family requires the Court to determine an appropriate custody and visitation time-share schedule. The question then before the Court is to determine what custody and visitation schedule is in the "best interests" of the child.

The scientific research literature from developmental psychology indicates that children benefit from having a complex relationship with both parents. Unless there are child abuse concerns, the goal of providing children with a full opportunity to develop a complex relationship with both parents would be in the best interests of the child's emotional and psychological development.

Children's healthy emotional and psychological development is also encouraged when they learn how to successfully resolve conflicts and restore relationships that have been damaged by prior conflict and family disagreement. Throughout their lives children will have to navigate interpersonal conflict, especially in their future families as adults, and learning the relationship and communication skills needed to repair conflict when it occurs is vital for the healthy development of children into successful and responsible adults. From the perspective of clinical psychology, when family conflicts emerge it is in the child's best interests to learn the communication and relationship skills needed to restore healthy, nurturing, and positive relationships within the family.

Healthy Child Development

Families contain four primary types of parent-child relationship; mother-son, mother-daughter, father-son, father-daughter. The benefits to the child from each of these relationship types is unique to that relationship, they are not replaceable or interchangeable in the value they provide to the child because each confers unique and vital developmental experiences that are immensely important for the child's healthy emotional and psychological development.

- **Mother-son bond:** The deep emotional and psychological connection between a male child and his mother is potentially one of the most affectionate parent-child bonding types. A positive and healthy mother-son bond creates for the child a deep inner sense of the child's inherent value as a person, and the mother-son bond forms the basis for the child's emotional security. The quality of the mother-son bond also establishes the template of expectations (the "internal working models") for the later formation of the child's spousal relationship in marriage.

- **Mother-daughter bond:** The mother-daughter bond can be one of the most complex parent-child relationships as the mother psychologically re-experiences herself and her own childhood in her daughter's development. The daughter draws important self-worth and gender identity modeling from a positive and healthy mother-daughter bond, and the mother-daughter bond serves as the template for the daughter's future role as a mother for her own children. Daughters become future mothers, and the relationship template formed in the mother-daughter bond carries important implications for the daughter's future parenting with her own children.

- **Father-son bond:** The son's emotional and psychological bond with the father provides essential self-esteem and gender identity modeling for the child. The son's healthy emotional and psychological bond to his father provides important communications of support from the father for the male child's sense of self-value as an emerging young man, and the son's bonded relationship with his father provides critical support for the child's development of the maturity that leads to the child entering the world as an emotionally mature and responsible young man.

- **Father-daughter bond:** A daughter's relationship with her father is one of the most affectionally important of the parent-child relationships. The daughter develops the core foundation for her self-worth from her affectionally bonded relationship with her father (an affectional process exemplified by the classic family roles as "daddy's princess" and "daddy's little girl"). As a primary relationship pattern, the father-daughter relationship also serves as the template (the "internal working model") that will guide the formation of her future spousal relationship with her own husband during marriage.

Each of these primary relationship types is unique, and the special value that each of these relationship types confer to the child is not interchangeable through the child's relationship with the other parent. The mother-son relationship offers a special loving warmth and richness in the child's development that is not interchangeable with the value offered to the son by the male-male affectional bond he has with his father. The father's relationship with his daughter is similarly filled with deep warmth and enriching love, and it is not interchangeable with the rich complexity of the mother-daughter bond. The child benefits from each of these unique relationships within the family, and each relationship type merits the full support of both parents and the Court in nourishing its development.

Divorce ends the spousal bond, but not the developmental benefits to the child from bonding to both parents. The mother-son bond is as vital and as important to the child's healthy development as the father-son bond, and the father-daughter relationship is equally important to the development of the child as the mother-daughter bond. Ensuring the child's ability to maintain a healthy and bonded relationship with both parents following divorce is critical to the child's healthy emotional and psychological development. In reaching custody visitation timeshare decisions following divorce, a shared 50-50% custody timeshare schedule provides the child with a full opportunity to develop a richly complex relationship with each parent. Limiting the child's opportunity to form any of these primary parent-child bonding opportunities will ultimately be damaging for the child's emotional and psychological development.

Attempting to compare the relative benefits received by the child from any of these primary relationship types is an impossible task. The scientific and professional literature in developmental and clinical psychology does not allow for a comparison of parenting to determine the "better parent" that would warrant truncating the child's opportunity to develop any of the entirely unique parent-child bonding relationships within the family. Each parent brings unique benefits from a complex relationship with the child that cannot be replaced or duplicated by the other parent. The unique developmental benefits that accrue from the son's relationship with his father is not interchangeable with the unique emotional and psychological benefits found in the son's bonded relationship with his mother. Similarly, the benefits to the daughter from an affectionally bonded relationship with her mother are unique to that relationship and are not interchangeable with the unique emotional and psychological benefits to the daughter acquired through her affectionate bond to her father. Each relationship type within the family - father-son; father-daughter; mother-son; mother-daughter - is unique, special, and critically important to the child's healthy development.

The scientific and professional literature contains no information that would allow professional psychology to render a scientifically or professionally supported opinion regarding the relative benefits of a 60-40%, 70-30%, 80-20%, or 90-10% custody visitation time-share schedule for any specific family situation. The parent-child relationship issues are simply too complex, the future is too variable, and such discriminations in the relative impact of these differing timeshare schedules are simply too fine grained to allow for a responsible professional position. Decisions on post-divorce custody and visitation schedules that favor the child's opportunity to form one type of complex parent-child relationship by truncating the child's opportunity to form a complex relationship type with the other parent will, of necessity, result in damage to the child's healthy emotional and psychological development by limiting the full richness of the child's developmental opportunity.

A post-divorce 50-50% custody timeshare schedule is the only responsible option that allows the child the full opportunity to develop a complex relationship with each parent. By equally valuing the unique richness for the child from each type of complex parent-child bond within the family, a 50-50% custody visitation schedule is the only option that is supported by the professional literature in developmental psychology. Childhood is a singular developmental process, and children pass through each developmental stage only once. Each developmental period of childhood is only available for a short period of time before the inevitability of maturation leads into a new developmental stage, and once lost, developmental opportunities during any phase of childhood are irretrievable. Special care needs to be taken in establishing post-divorce custody visitation schedules to ensure that the child has a full developmental opportunity within childhood to form a complex and healthy relationship with each parent, recognizing the special and unique role of each type of parent-child primary bond.

Within professional psychology, the only professional opinion that would be supported by the scientific and professional literature is that children benefit from a complex relationship with both parents. The goal of fostering the child's healthy development of a complex relationship with each parent will benefit from a balanced 50-50% custody timeshare schedule that provides the child with a full opportunity to form a unique and complex relationship with each parent. Truncating the child's opportunity to form a unique and complex relationship with either parent will inherently rob the child of the richness available from that parent-child relationship.

From the perspective of the child development literature, deviations from a balanced post-divorce 50-50% shared visitation schedule only become warranted in response to child abuse concerns, in which child protection considerations take precedence over the harm created to a foundational parent-child bond from a truncated parent-child bonding opportunity; from a restricted father-son; father-daughter; mother-son; mother-daughter bond during childhood. In the absence of child abuse concerns, the only child custody and visitation timeshare schedule that is supported by the scientific and professional literature is a balanced 50-50% custody timeshare that provides the child with the opportunity to develop a complex relationship with both parents. Parents are free to cooperatively decide on alternative custody timeshare schedules that best fit their family circumstances. But when parents cannot reach a cooperative co-parenting agreement on a shared custody visitation schedule, then the only scientifically and professional supported custody timeshare schedule would be to value the benefits for the child inherent to each of the parent-child relationship types within the family. The father-son/mother-son bonds are unique and equally valuable, as are the father-daughter/mother-daughter relationships. No relationship type should be given primacy, and in the absence of child abuse concerns, no relationship opportunity for the child should be truncated.

The "Custody Prize"

Parents have the inherent right to make collaborative decisions on their cooperative co-parenting following divorce, including deciding on custody visitation schedules that best fit for their unique family circumstances. However, when parents are unable to collaborate in reaching a decision on a shared custody visitation schedule, then this decision falls to the Court.

When parents cannot cooperatively agree on a custody time-share schedule, efforts by the Court and professional psychology to then determine which parent is the "better parent" who should be awarded a larger share of custody time with the child will not only damage the child's opportunity to form a complex relationship with each parent (the father-daughter; father-son; mother-daughter; mother-son relationship), but any efforts by professional psychology or the Court to determine the "better parent" who should be awarded a larger share of child custody time with the child will effectively turn the child into a "custody prize" to be "won" in the spousal dispute surrounding the divorce by the supposedly "better parent," thereby encouraging each parent to then compete for the child.

Turning the child into a "custody prize" to be awarded to the supposedly "better parent" will have an extremely destructive and corrosive effect on the family's ability to transition from the pre-divorce intact family structure to a healthy post-divorce separated family structure of shared co-parenting. Turning the child into a "custody prize" to be won by the supposedly "better parent" will create a family environment in which the child becomes *triangulated* into the spousal conflict as a proxy source of spousal conflict. The immense danger that develops from trying to determine the "better parent" is that one parent will then compete for the designation as the "better parent" by enlisting the child into a *cross-generational coalition* with this parent against the other parent, creating a "good-parent"/"bad-parent" (favored parent/unfavored parent) dichotomy within the family that destroys the child's opportunity to develop a healthy complex relationship with each parent (a healthy mother-son; mother-daughter; father-son; father-daughter relationship). By turning the child into a "custody prize" for the supposedly "better parent," the child becomes a surrogate in the inter-spousal conflict and the child's authentic individual relationships with each parent will be undermined and ultimately damaged by the parental competition to be the "favored parent" who will be designated the "better parent" ("better person") who will be awarded the "custody prize" of the child.

Whenever there is prominent spousal conflict surrounding divorce, turning the child into a "custody prize" to be won through litigation, psychological evaluation, and the child's expressed preferences for a parent is not in the child's best interests. Following divorce, children benefit from remaining completely neutral family members in their parents' spousal conflict. Children's neutrality is preserved by not turning them into "prizes to be won" by the supposedly "better parent" (by the "better person"/"better spouse") following the divorce. Guarding children's absolute neutrality in their parents' spousal conflict allows the children to maintain an affectional bond to each parent and supports the child's development of a healthy complex relationship with each parent (the unique father-daughter; father-son; mother-daughter; mother-son relationship). Children should not be asked to take sides, nor should they be allowed to be covertly influenced by a parent into taking sides. Children are neutral. Turning the child into a "custody prize" to be won by the supposedly "better parent" creates a destructive and deeply corrosive force within the family that undermines the ability to maintain the child's neutrality within the spousal conflict.

Attachment Conflict

Once the Court decides on a custody time-share schedule, problems can emerge in enacting the Court-ordered custody visitation schedule if the child develops significant conflict with one parent (such as the child's expressed hostility and rejection toward a parent) that then creates a cutoff in the child's bond to that parent. The emergence of family conflict following the divorce of the child's parents is a treatment-related issue, not a custody-related issue.

Except in cases of child abuse, establishing a shared 50-50% custody visitation schedule is in the child's developmental best interests by allowing the child a full opportunity to form a complex relationship with each parent; the father-son bond, the mother-son bond, the father-daughter bond, the mother-daughter bond. If parent-child conflict is interfering with enacting a normal-range shared custody visitation schedule, this is a family treatment issue to be resolved in family therapy. The causes and solutions to family conflict are the domain of family therapy, not litigation, and should be resolved in therapy, not through repeated litigation.

A child's rejection of a parent is fundamentally an ***attachment-related*** pathology. The attachment system is the brain system that governs all aspects of love and bonding throughout the lifespan, including grief and loss. The attachment system is a neurologically embedded primary motivational system of the brain. The parent-child bond represents a primary attachment bond. The spousal relationship represents a secondary attachment bond that forms later in life and uses patterns of attachment bonding formed in the primary attachment relationships of childhood. The parent-child attachment bond is the foundational relationship around which the attachment system developed across millions of years of evolution. Children who formed strong attachment bonds to parents received parental protection from predators, thereby increasing their chances for survival and increasing the genes that motivated these children's strong attachment bonding to parents in the collective gene pool. On the othe hand, children who formed weaker attachment bonds to their parents would fall prey to predators and other environmental dangers at higher rates, and their genes motivating them to form weaker attachment bonds to their parents would be systematically and selectively removed from the collective gene pool.

Through the evolutionary pressures applied by the selective predation of children and the survival advantage attachment bonding provided to children, a very strong and highly resilient *primary motivational system* developed in the brain (the attachment system) that powerfully motivates children to form strong attachment bonds to their parents. As a primary motivational system of the brain, the attachment system functions in characteristic ways, and it dysfunctions in characteristic ways. Because of the significant survival advantage conferred to children by forming an attachment bond to their parents, the attachment system is a "goal-corrected" motivational system, meaning that it <u>always</u> seeks the goal of forming an attachment bond to the parent. In response to bad parenting, the attachment system changes <u>how</u> the child seeks to form an attached bond to the parent, but it always maintains the *goal* of forming an attachment bond to the parent.

The attachment system <u>always</u> motivates children to form an attachment bond to the parent, even to bad parents, because the attachment system is a *goal-corrected* motivational system that changes how the child tries to bond to the parent but always maintains the *goal* of forming an attachment bond to the parent. This is true even when parents are problematic in their parenting. The attachment system does not allow the child to reject a bad parent. Instead, the attachment system MORE strongly motivates the child to bond to the bad parent. To understand why children are more strongly motivated to bond to bad parents, requires an understanding for how the attachment system developed through the evolutionary pressures from the selective predation of children.

Within the context of evolution, problematic parenting more fully exposes children to the risks posed by predators and other environmental dangers. Children who had bad parents were more likely to be eaten by predators, were more likely to die from a myriad of environmental dangers, and were more likely to die from neglect and starvation. Children of bad parents died at higher rates, and any children who rejected bad parents became even more likely to fall prey to predators and to die from other environmental dangers. Because rejecting bad parents significantly increased the mortality rates of children, over the course of millions of years of evolution genes that motivated children to reject bad parents were systematically eliminated from the collective gene pool.

On the other hand, children whose attachment system MORE strongly motivated them to form an attachment bond to the bad parent would be more likely to acquire parental protection from predators and parental care because of the child's increased motivation and effort to form an attachment bond to the problematic parent. Children who became more strongly motivated to bond to a bad parent were more likely to survive, thereby increasing their genes in the collective gene pool for more strongly motivating children to form an attachment bond to a problematic parent. The increased child motivation to bond to a problematic parent is called an "insecure attachment," and scientific research has identified several patterns to insecure attachment, all of which are designed to maximize parental involvement with the child. As a primary motivational system of the brain, the attachment system functions in characteristic ways, and it dysfunctions in characteristic ways.

The attachment system is a *goal-corrected* motivational system that more strongly motivates children to form an attachment bond to a bad and problematic parent. The attachment system does not motivate children to reject a bad parent. Instead it changes HOW the child tries to form an attachment bond to the parent. The patterns of insecure attachment (the patterns for the how the child seeks to form an attached bond to a problematic parent) have been extensively investigated in the scientific research literature. A child's chronic conflict with a parent represents one pattern of insecure attachment in which the child's increased "protest behavior" (chronic conflict with the parent) is designed to elicit increased parental involvement. The *goal-corrected* motivations of the child's attachment networks are motivating the child to bond with the problematic parent, but some aspect of the parent's problematic parenting is preventing the child from forming of a secure attachment bond to the parent, leading to the child's "protest behavior" expressed through the parent-child conflict. Attachment-related parent-child conflict emerges from the increased motivation of the child's attachment networks to form an attachment bond to the parent which is being prevented by some aspect of problematic parenting by the parent. The child's continuing motivation to form a parent-child bond and the child's frustrated ability of the child to form an affectionally bonded relationship with the parent is the causal origin the chronic parent-child conflict.

Treatment of attachment-related pathology that is creating parent-child conflict involves identifying the parenting practices that are interfering with the child's ability to form an attached bond to the parent, and then by changing these parenting practices the child's attachment bonding motivation is allowed to find completion in the formation of an affectionally bonded relationship with the parent. Children always want to form an attached bond to the parent because that is the way the attachment system (a primary motivational system of the brain) works. Parent-child conflict emerges when there is a barrier to the child forming an attached bond to the parent. Therapy involves identifying and removing the barrier to bonding to allow the child's normal-range attachment motivations to find completion in a bonded relationship to the parent.

Children never reject a parent, not even a problematic parent. Problematic parenting MORE strongly motivates the child to form an attachment bond to the parent. Chronic parent-child conflict is created by the frustration of the child's desire to bond to the parent. Remove the barrier to bonding and the child's natural attachment bonding motivations will restore the parent-child bond. A child's motivated rejection of a parent (a "detachment behavior") is an extremely aberrant and inauthentic display of the attachment system.

Pathogenic Parenting

Since the attachment system confers such significant survival advantage to children, the attachment system <u>never</u> spontaneously dysfunctions. If the attachment system were to spontaneously dysfunction, this would increase the child's exposure to survival risks by interfering with the child's attachment bonding to the parent. The attachment system only becomes dysfunctional in response to *pathogenic parenting* (patho=pathology; genic=genesis, creation). Pathogenic parenting is the creation of significant pathology in the child through aberrant and distorted parenting practices. Pathogenic parenting is an established construct in both developmental and clinical psychology and it is typically used in reference to attachment-related pathology, since the attachment system never spontaneously dysfunctions but only becomes dysfunctional in response to pathogenic parenting. The development of attachment-related pathology in the child is always the product of pathogenic parenting.

Attachment-related pathology evidenced by the child is therefore a clear symptom indication of *pathogenic parenting* (of severely problematic parenting creating significant psychopathology in the child) by one parent or the other. Either the child's attachment-related pathology is being created by the pathogenic parenting of the targeted-rejected parent through significantly abusive parenting practices (such as through chronic and severe physical abuse of the child or through parental sexual abuse of the child), or by the pathogenic parenting of the allied and supposedly "favored" parent who has formed a *cross-generational coalition* with the child against the other parent (Goldenberg & Goldenberg, 2013; Haley 1977; Minuchin, 1974)[1]

The attachment bonding motivation confers such significant survival advantage to the child that the degree of pathogenic parenting required by the targeted-rejected parent to terminate the child's attachment-bonding motivations toward that parent would need to be in the severe forms of child abuse that are of sufficient intensity to terminate a primary motivational system of the brain that is strongly motivating the child's bonding to the parent. Lesser forms of problematic parenting will create an *insecure attachment* that MORE strongly motivates the child to bond to the problematic parent. Because attachment bonding to the parent confers such significant survival advantage to the child, only severely abusive parenting practices by the targeted-rejected parent will terminate the child's attachment bonding motivations toward the parent.

Attachment-related pathology involving the suppression of the child's attachment bonding motivations toward the targeted-rejected parent can also be caused by the pathogenic parenting of the allied and supposedly "favored" parent who has formed a *cross-generational coalition* with the child against the other parent. The formation of a cross-generational coalition with one parent against the other parent is extensively described in the family systems literature

---

[1] Goldenberg H, Goldenberg I. (2013). Family therapy: An overview. 8th ed. Florence, KY: Brooks/Cole Publishing/Cengage Learning.

Haley, J. (1977). Toward a theory of pathological systems. In P. Watzlawick & J. Weakland (Eds.), The interactional view (pp. 31-48). New York: Norton.

Minuchin, S. (1974). Families and family therapy. Harvard University Press.

and involves *triangulating* the child into the spousal conflict (placing the child in the middle of the spousal conflict), and using the child either as a weapon against the other spouse/(parent) or the child is used by the allied parent to stabilize the fragile emotional structure of this parent that is collapsing surrounding the divorce (such as to alleviate this parent's fears of abandonment that were triggered by the divorce).

Family systems therapy is one of the primary schools of psychotherapy (the others being psychoanalytic, cognitive-behavioral, and humanistic-existential therapy). Of the primary schools of psychotherapy, only family systems therapy deals with resolving the complex interpersonal relationships within families, all of the other models of psychotherapy are more individually focused forms of psychotherapy. Family systems therapy and family systems constructs therefore provide the appropriate diagnostic and treatment-related framework for understanding and treating family-related pathology. The child's *triangulation* into the spousal conflict through the formation of a *cross-generational coalition* with the child against the other parent is a fully recognized and fully described family relationship dynamic in family systems therapy in which the child's hostility toward the targeted parent is being covertly created by the negative parent influence on the child by the allied parent in order to meet the emotional and psychological needs of the allied parent.

Triangulation

When spousal conflict becomes excessive, a third party, often the child, will be incorporated into the spousal conflict to help stablize the dysfunctional spousal relationship. Incorporating the child into the spousal conflict is referred to as "triangulating" the child into the spousal conflict because it turns the two-person spouse-spouse conflict into a three-person, spouse-child-spouse, triangular conflict with the child caught in the middle. The child's trianguation into the spousal conflict is created by one parent who coerces or manipulates the child into "choosing sides" in the spousal conflict, forming a cross-generational coalition with the child against the other parent.

The cross-generational coalition with one parent against the other parent violates the child's neutrality in the spousal conflict and creates a distinctive "favored parent"/"disfavored parent" dichotomy in the family. The hostility created toward the targeted parent by the cross-generational coalition with the allied and supposedly "favored" parent acts to feed the narcissistic self-esteem of the allied parent as being the supposedly "favored" and "better" parent (person), and the allied parent's own spousal anger toward the other spouse/(parent) takes a sadistic satisfaction in the child's ongoing conflict with the targeted-rejected parent and the suffering caused to this parent in revenge and retaliation for the divorce.

Assessing and identifying the family pathology of a cross-generational coalition can be challenging because it is typically a hidden form of family pathology in which the allied parent's influence on the child is subtle, and it is concealed beneath the child's manipulated assertion of independent beliefs and action. In his description of the cross-generational coalition, the renowned family systems therapist, Jay Haley, describes the hidden nature of the pathology that "there is a certain behavior which indicates a coalition" but that when this behavior is identified as a coalition, "the coalition will be denied."

"The people responding to each other in the triangle are not peers, but one of them is of a different generation from the other two... In the process of their interaction together, the person of one generation forms a coalition with the person of the other generation against his peer. By 'coalition' is meant a process of joint action which is *against* the third person... The coalition between the two persons is denied. That is, there is certain behavior which indicates a coalition which, when it is queried, will be denied as a coalition... In essence, the perverse triangle is one in which the separation of generations is breached in a covert way. When this occurs as a repetitive pattern, the system will be pathological." (Haley, 1977, p. 37)[2]

The parent-child conflict with the targeted parent is being superficially blamed on the bad parenting of the targeted-rejected parent, but is actually being created by the manipulative influence and psychological control of the child by the allied and supposedly "favored" parent who has formed a covert and psychologically manipulative cross-generational coalition with the child against the other parent. In their book, *Family Healing*,[3] the preeminent family systems therapist Salvador Minuchin and his co-author, Michael Nichols, provide a structural family diagram for a cross-generational coalition between a father and son that excludes the mother. The cross-generational coalition of the child with the father empowers the child into an elevated position in the family hierarchy above the mother from which the child feels entitled to judge the adequacy of the mother as a parent and person. The child's elevated status in the family is called an "inverted family hierarchy" and is created by the empowerment of the child by the allied parent in a cross-generational coalition with the child

Diagram of a cross-generational coalition, inverted hierarchy, and enmeshment
(Minuchin & Nichols, 1993, p. 42)

In normal and healthy families, parents occupy the position of executive leadership in the family from which parents judge their children's behavior as appropriate or inappropriate, and the parents then deliver consequences (rewards and punishments) based on parental judgements of their children's behavior. In an ***inverted family hierarchy***, however, this natural and healthy family structure of parental executive leadership is turned upside-down, so that the child becomes over-empowered by the support and covert coalition with the allied parent to the point of feeling entitled to judge the adequacy of the targeted-rejected parent. From this elevated position in the family hierarchy, the child then feels entitled to deliver punishments (such as hostility and rejection of the parent) to the targeted parent based on the child's judgement of this parent's inadequacy.

The three lines between the father and child in this structural family diagram indicate an "enmeshed" psychological relationship of over-involvement between the allied parent and child. The term "enmeshment" refers to the loss of psychological boundaries between the

---

[2] Haley, J. (1977). Toward a theory of pathological systems. In P. Watzlawick & J. Weakland (Eds.), The interactional view (pp. 31-48). New York: Norton.

[3] Minuchin. S. & Nichols, M.P. (1993). Family healing: Strategies for hope and understanding. New York: Touchstone.

family members so that the enmeshed family members share must share the same identical attitudes and beliefs in order to maintain their bonded relationship. In a cross-generational coalition, the psychological enmeshment of the child with the allied parent creates a same-mind presentation of identical parent-child attitudes and beliefs, centered primarily on the supposed inadequacy of the targeted-rejected parent.

In his foundational book on family therapy, *Families and Family Therapy*,[4] Minuchin provides a clinical example of the effects of a cross-generational coalition on family relationships following divorce:

> "An inappropriately rigid cross-generational subsystem of mother and son versus father appears, and the boundary around this coalition of mother and son excludes the father. A cross-generational dysfunctional transactional pattern has developed." (Minuchin, 1974, p. 61-62)

> "The parents were divorced six months earlier and the father is now living alone… Two of the children who were very attached to their father, now refuse any contact with him. The younger children visit their father but express great unhappiness with the situation." (Minuchin, p. 101)

Through the covert support provided to the child through the cross-generational coalition with the allied parent, the child becomes empowered to defy both the authority of the other parent and of the Court. In post-divorce families with continuing custody-related conflicts, the child's over-empowerment is revealed in the child's overt defiance of the Court's authority in establishing the custody visitation schedule for the family by refusing to abide by the Court-ordered custody visitation schedule. In some cases, the child may threaten to run-away from the targeted parent or the child may threaten self-harm if the child is "forced" to cooperate with the authority of the Court, revealing the child's over-empowered effort to impose the child's will upon the Court's decisions.

The over-empowerment of the child is created through the tacit approval and "understanding" the child's conflict with the targeted parent receives from the allied and supposedly "favored" parent. The allied parent adopts a "protective parent" role of "understanding" for the child's position of defiance, and the allied parent evidences a selective parental incompetence by declining to exercise parental authority with the child ("What can I do, I can't force the child to go on visitations with the other parent"). Instead of exercising appropriate parental guidance and authority, the allied parent adopts a stance of deferring to the child's wishes ("The child should be allowed to decide…") that empowers the child and places the child in a position to choose sides in the spousal-divorce conflict by identifying a "favored" and "disfavored" parent (thereby violating the child's neutrality in the spousal conflict surrounding the divorce). The subtly hidden and concealed support the child receives from the allied parent for the child's conflict with the other parent is typically evidenced by the allied parent offering displays of rationalizing justifications and supportive "understanding" for the child's conflicts with the other parent. The child is manipulatively placed out front in creating conflict with the targeted parent, while the manipulative influence of the allied parent

---

[4] Minuchin, S. (1974). Families and family therapy. Harvard University Press.

remains concealed behind protestations of selective parental incompetence ("What can I do, I can't force the child to…") and parental displays of support for the child's empowerment ("We need to listen to what the child wants…") when the child's expressed wishes have been created by the manipulative influence of the allied parent.

In severely dysfunctional family relationships, the hostility created between the child and targeted parent can lead to an "emotional cutoff" (Bowen, 1978; Titelman, 2003)[5] in the child's relationship with the targeted parent, in which the child seeks to completely terminate the child's relationship with the targeted-rejected parent. Minuchin and Nichols (1993) also provide a structural family diagram for the relationship cutoff created by a cross-generational coalition (in this example, of a father and the son against the mother). This diagram from their book, *Family Healing*, graphically illustrates that the cross-generational coalition of the father with the child creates both an *inverted family hierarchy* in which the child is empowered by the *cross-generational coalition* into an elevated position of judgement above the mother, and also creates an *emotional cutoff* in which the mother is rejected by the father-son psychologically enmeshed coalition.

Cross-generational coalition & cutoff
(Minuchin & Nichols, 1993, p. 42)

The formation of a cross-generational coalition with the child against the other parent results from either, or both, of two primary causes in the motivational agenda of the allied parent:

1.) **Diverting Spousal Anger**: The allied parent is using the coalition with the child to divert the allied parent's own anger toward the other spouse through the child. The child is essentially being "weaponized" into the spousal conflict by the manipulative influence and psychological control of the child by the allied parent who is using the child as a surrogate proxy for the expression of the allied parent's own spousal anger toward the other spouse surrounding their divorce.

2.) **Allaying Abandonment Fears**: The allied parent is first creating and then covertly supporting the child's ongoing conflict with the targeted-rejected parent as a means of maintaining sole "possession" of the child in order to allay the allied parent's own fears of abandonment that were triggered by the divorce (or by the remarriage of the other parent). In this motivational agenda, the allied parent fears that if the child is allowed to love the other parent then the child will not love (will abandon) the allied parent.

---

[5] Bowen, M. (1978). Family therapy in clinical practice. New York: Jason Aronson.

Titelman, P. (2003). Emotional cutoff: Bowen family systems theory perspectives. New York: The Hawthorn Press, Inc.

Assessing for Pathogenic Parenting

Attachment-related pathology is always created by pathogenic parenting. The issue of professional concern in assessing attachment-related pathology that emerges surrounding divorce is identifying the source of the *pathogenic parenting* that is creating the child's attachment-related pathology. The pathogenic parenting is by either the targeted-rejected parent through significantly abusive parenting practices, or the pathogenic parenting is by the allied parent and supposedly "favored" parent who has formed a cross-generational coalition with the child against the other parent. These are the only two possible causal origins for the child's attachment-related pathology surrounding the divorce.

A treatment-focused assessment of attachment-related pathology surrounding divorce represents a targeted and focused clinical assessment of the attachment-related pathology evidenced by the child, that has its specific purpose identifying which parent represents the causal source of the pathogenic parenting that is creating the child's pathology (either the pathogenic parenting by the targeted-rejected parent or the pathogenic parenting by the allied and supposedly "favored" parent).

Assessing the causal origins of pathology involves a process of *differential diagnosis* in which the information is systematically collected to evaluate the various alternative causal possibilities that could be creating the specific features of the displayed symptoms. The differential diagnosis for attachment-related pathology involves systematically collecting information regarding the potentially pathogenic parenting of each parent. At the beginning of the differential diagnostic process, all of the possible causal origins for the symptoms are considered. Relevant information is then systematically collected that will eliminate some diagnostic possibilities from consideration, or that provides a constellation of support for other diagnostic possibilities, until only a single diagnostic possibility remains and diagnostic clarity is achieved in identifying the causal origins of the child's pathology.

Assessing the Targeted Parent

The process of differential diagnosis for the source of pathogenic parenting creating attachment-related pathology begins with the documenting the assessment of the targeted parent's parenting practices. The attachment system is a neurologically embedded primary motivational system of the brain that strongly motivates children to form an attached and affectionally bonded relationship to parents, even with problematic parents. In response to problematic parenting, the child's attachment system (a neurologically embedded primary motivational system of the brain) <u>MORE</u> strongly motivates the child to form an attached bond to the parent, called an "insecure attachment."

As discussed earlier, since the attachment system is a *goal-corrected* motivational system it always maintains the goal of forming an affectionally attached bond to the parent. In response to problematic parenting, the attachment system changes HOW the child seeks to form an attached bond to the parent (such as through displays of high-protest attention-seeking behaviors, or through low-demand self-sufficiency), but the attachment system <u>always</u> maintains the goal of forming an attachment bond to the parent. If pathogenic parenting by the targeted-rejected parent is creating the parent-child conflict, then identifying and resolving the problematic parenting behavior that is preventing the child from forming an attachment bond to the parent will remove the barrier to the parent-child bonding, which will then allow the normal-range functioning of the child's attachment system to find completion in the creation of a healthy and bonded parent-child relationship.

In a treatment-focused assessment of attachment-related pathology surrounding divorce, the assessment of potential pathogenic parenting by the targeted-rejected parent is guided and documented using the *Parenting Practices Rating Scale* (Appendix 1). The structure of the *Parenting Practices Rating Scale* provides a categorical identification of the parenting practices by the targeted-rejected parent into four categories moving from highly pathological parenting to normal-range and healthy parenting:

Category 1: Child Abuse

Category 2: Severely Problematic Parenting

Category 3: Somewhat Problematic but Normal-Range Parenting

Category 4: Positive and Healthy Parenting

Following this categorical rating, the *Parenting Practices Rating Scale* then documents a rating of parenting practices along a 0-100 scale, from neglectful-uninvolved parenting at one end of the spectrum to hostile-controlling parenting at the other end. A clinical rating of parental empathy is then made along a continuum from absent empathy to intrusive over-involvement, and the Parenting Practices Rating Scale concludes by identifying domains of clinical concern for potentially problematic parental pathology and substance abuse concerns.

The *Parenting Practices Rating Scale* is an assessment documentation instrument that both guides and documents the collection of information regarding the parenting practices of the targeted-rejected parent. If areas of problematic parenting are identified regarding the parenting practices of the targeted-rejected parent, then the specific areas of problematic of parenting become documented by the *Parenting Practices Rating Scale* and can then become the focus of family therapy. Once these identified areas of problematic parenting are resolved, then the normal-range expression of the child's attachment bonding motivation toward the targeted parent will be allowed to complete its goal of forming an attached bond to the parent.

Assessing the Allied Parent

A treatment-focused assessment for pathogenic parenting by the allied and supposedly "favored" parent is a targeted assessment for a possible cross-generational coalition of the allied parent with the child against the targeted parent. A cross-generational coalition can be more difficult to identify because the allied parent is concealing the parent's manipulative influence and psychological control of the child behind the child's supposedly independent decision to reject the other parent.

Parental psychological control of the child has received extensive validation in the scientific literature. In his book, *Intrusive Parenting: How Psychological Control Affects Children and Adolescents* (2002),[6] published by the American Psychological Association, Brian Barber and his colleague, Elizabeth Harmon (Barber & Harmon, 2002),[7] cite over 30 empirically validated scientific studies that measure the construct of parental psychological control of the child. Barber and Harmon offer the following definition of parental psychological control of the child;

> "Psychological control refers to parental behaviors that are intrusive and manipulative of children's thoughts, feelings, and attachment to parents. These behaviors appear to be associated with disturbances in the psychoemotional boundaries between the child and parent, and hence with the development of an independent sense of self and identity." (Barber & Harmon, 2002, p. 15)

Stone, Buehler, and Barber (2002)[8] describe the process by which the parent exerts psychological control over the child thoughts and feelings;

> "Parental psychological control is defined as verbal and nonverbal behaviors that intrude on youth's emotional and psychological autonomy… The central elements of psychological control are intrusion into the child's psychological world and self-definition and parental attempts to manipulate the child's thoughts and feelings through invoking guilt, shame, and anxiety. Psychological control is distinguished from behavioral control in that the parent attempts to control, through the use of criticism, dominance, and anxiety or guilt induction, the youth's thoughts and feelings rather than the youth's behavior." (Stone, Buehler, and Barber, 2002, p. 57)

---

[6] Barber, B. K. (Ed.) (2002). Intrusive parenting: How psychological control affects children and adolescents. Washington, DC: American Psychological Association.

[7] Barber, B. K. and Harmon, E. L. (2002). Violating the self: Parenting psychological control of children and adolescents. In B. K. Barber (Ed.), Intrusive parenting (pp. 15-52). Washington, DC: American Psychological Association.

[8] Stone, G., Buehler, C., & Barber, B. K. (2002) Interparental conflict, parental psychological control, and youth problem behaviors. In B. K. Barber (Ed.), Intrusive parenting: How psychological control affects children and adolescents. Washington, D.C.: American Psychological Association.

Soenens and Vansteenkiste (2010)[9] describe the various methods used by parents to achieve psychological control of the child:

> "Psychological control can be expressed through a variety of parental tactics, including (a) guilt-induction, which refers to the use of guilt inducing strategies to pressure children to comply with a parental request; (b) contingent love or love withdrawal, where parents make their attention, interest, care, and love contingent upon the children's attainment of parental standards; (c) instilling anxiety, which refers to the induction of anxiety to make children comply with parental requests; and (d) invalidation of the child's perspective, which pertains to parental constraining of the child's spontaneous expression of thoughts and feelings." (Soenens & Vansteenkiste, 2010, p. 75)

The Narcissistic-Borderline Parent

Of prominent clinical concern in the assessment of attachment-related pathology surrounding divorce is the potential for a cross-generational coalition of the child with a narcissistic and/or borderline personality parent who is using the child's hostility and rejection of the other parent to stabilize this parent's own fragile personality structure that is being threatened with collapse surrounding the inherent rejection and abandonment by the spousal attachment figure surround the divorce (Childress, 2015).[10]

Narcissistic personality pathology is particularly vulnerable to collapse in response to rejection. The spousal rejection inherent to divorce would trigger the narcissistic vulnerability of this parent, called a "narcissistic injury." The narcissistic spouse would then retaliate for the spousal rejection of the divorce by triangulating the child into the spousal conflict and then using and exploiting the child as a weapon of revenge against the other spouse in retaliation for the narcissistic injury of spousal rejection surrounding the divorce.

Borderline personality pathology is especially vulnerable to their fears of abandonment. These abandonment fears would similarly be triggered by the loss of the spousal attachment figure surrounding divorce. In response to the perceived abandonment created by the divorce, a borderline personality parent will seek triangulate the child into the spousal conflict in order to obtain sole possession of the of the child in order to allay and counteract this parent's fears of abandonment. The excessive anxiety at separation and fear of abandonment experienced by the borderline personality parent would be transferred to the child as displays of excessive anxiety at separation from the borderline parent, reassuring the borderline parent of the child's devotion, leading the child to protest visitation with the other parent, and ultimately to refuse visitations with the other parent.

---

[9] Soenens, B. and Vansteenkiste, M. (2010). A theoretical upgrade of the concept of parental psychological control: Proposing new insights on the basis of self-determination theory. Developmental Review, 30, 74–99.

[10] Childress, C.A. (2015). An attachment-based model of parental alienation: Foundations. Claremont, CA; Oaksong Press.

The differential diagnosis is to identify the source of pathogenic parenting that is creating the child's attachment-related pathology by determining which parent is creating the child's symptomatic hostility and rejection of the targeted parent. Since pathogenic parenting is the creation of child's pathology, the pathogenic parenting will leave telltale evidence ("psychological fingerprints") of the parent's psychological control and manipulation of the child in the child's symptom display. It is through these telltale symptom indicators in the child's symptom display of the child's psychological control and manipulation by a narcissistic/(borderline) parent that the pathogenic parenting by an allied narcissistic and/or borderline personality parent can be identified.

Pathogenic parenting by an allied narcissistic/(borderline) parent who has formed a cross-generational coalition with the child against the other parent will leave a characteristic set of three diagnostic indicators in the child's symptom display:

1. **Attachment Symptoms:** The child's symptoms will evidence a prominent suppression in the child's normal-range attachment bonding motivations toward a normal-range and affectionally available parent. The attachment system is a goal-corrected motivational system that always seeks the goal of forming an attached bond to the parent. A child rejecting a normal-range and affectionally available parent (as assessed and documented by the *Parenting Practices Rating Scale*, would represent the clinical evidence of an inauthentic (artificially influenced) display of the child's attachment system.

2. **Narcissistic Symptoms:** Psychological control of the child by a narcissistic/(borderline) parent will leave "psychological fingerprint" evidence of this control in the child's symptom display. When a child is being psychologically influence and controlled by a narcissistic/(borderline) parent, the child's symptoms will evidence a characteristic set of five narcissistic personality traits displayed selectively toward the targeted-rejected parent. The origin of these narcissistic symptoms displayed by the child toward the targeted-rejected parent are from the psychological manipulation and control of the child by the allied narcissistic/(borderline) parent who is the source of these narcissistic attitudes toward the other spouse. The child is acquiring the attitudes and personality pathology of the allied narcissistic/(borderline) parent toward the other spouse/parent through the psychological manipulation and control of the child by the allied narcissistic/(borderline) parent.

3. **Delusional False Belief:** The child will evidence a fixed and false belief that is maintained despite contrary evidence (a delusion) that the child is being "victimized" by the normal-range parenting of the targeted-rejected parent (an encapsulated persecutory delusion). This symptom feature is evidence of a childhood attachment trauma reenactment narrative of the narcissistic/(borderline) parent that is being recreated into the current family relationships in a false trauma pattern of "abusive parent"/"victimized child"/"protective parent." This is a false narrative that is being created from the childhood attachment trauma of the narcissistic/(borderline) parent, embedded in the "internal working models" (schemas) of this parent's attachment networks. The presence of this false belief narrative in the child's symptom display toward the targeted parent is clinical evidence for the influence on the child by an allied

narcissistic/(borderline) parent, who is the actual source origin for this false persecutory belief system.

If all three of these symptoms are evidenced in the child's symptom display, then there is no other pathology in all of mental health that could produce this specific set of three child symptoms other than pathogenic parenting by an allied narcissistic/(borderline) personality parent who has formed a cross-generational coalition with the child against the other parent. The presence in the child's symptom display of all three of these symptoms represents definitive diagnostic evidence for pathogenic parenting by an allied narcissistic/(borderline) parent. The *Diagnostic Checklist for Pathogenic Parenting* (Appendix 2) documents the assessment for these three symptoms, along with documenting an additional set of Associated Clinical Signs that frequently co-occur through the pathogenic parenting of an allied narcissistic/(borderline) parent.

The *Diagnostic Checklist for Pathogenic Parenting* represents a symptom documentation instrument that establishes pathogenic parenting by an allied narcissistic/(borderline) parent who is triangulating the child into the spousal conflict by creating a cross-generational coalition with the child against the other parent.

Session Protocol

A treatment-focused assessment protocol represents a targeted clinical assessment to determine the causal source of pathogenic parenting creating the child's attachment-related pathology surrounding divorce. The session structure protocol for a treatment-focused assessment of pathogenic parenting is through a six-session semi-structured targeted assessment protocol in three phases. Each phase consists of two 90-minute clinical assessment sessions.

Phase 1: The first phase of assessment is with each parent individually to collect history and symptom information and begin the differential diagnostic process.

Phase 2: The second phase is a direct assessment of the child's symptom display through meetings with the child and in conjoint parent-child sessions with the child and targeted parent.

Phase 3: The third phase provides feedback to each parent to assess the organizing "schema patterns" of each parent surrounding the child's symptom display.

In some families, the complexity of the family background history and symptom information may be extensive and require additional initial assessment sessions with each parent individually to collect sufficient background information to identify the child's symptom features and the surrounding family context for the child's symptoms. In some cases, additional direct assessment sessions of the child's relationship with the targeted-rejected parent may be necessary to achieve clarity in the child's active symptom display.

- **Initial Parent Sessions**

    The assessment protocol begins with two 90-minute clinical interviews with each parent individually to collect history and symptom information from each parent's perspective. The content covered in these sessions includes:

    - A description of the child's symptoms from each parent's perspective.

    - The onset of child symptoms and the surrounding family context.

    - The attributions of causality offered by each parent for the child's symptoms.

- **Direct Assessment**

    The middle two sessions are a direct assessment of the child's symptom display.

    In older children or when the child symptom display is of excessive anxiety surrounding the targeted parent, an individual clinical interview session with only the child may begin this phase of direct clinical assessment. At least one dyadic parent-child session is conducted for direct observation of the child's symptoms and relationship features with the targeted-rejected parent.

    During this direct assessment, the interactional features displayed in the parent-child conflict will evidence either problematic parenting features of insecure attachment (authentic parent-child conflict) or symptom features of a cross-generational coalition with an allied parent against the targeted parent (inauthentic parent-child conflict).

    Response-to-intervention probes during the parent-child session and establishing the behavior-chain sequence for the parent-child conflict s will help reveal the origins of the child's attachment-related symptoms as being caused either by the problematic parenting of the targeted-rejected parent or by a cross-generational coalition with the allied parent.

- **Assessment of Parent Response:**

    The final two sessions are clinical feedback sessions provided to each parent individually to assess the "schema patterns"[11] of each parent in response to the clinical findings from the assessment sessions. The clinical information obtained in these two final sessions with each parent individually is used to confirm the differential diagnostic evidence displayed during the prior assessment sessions.

---

[11] Schemas: "How a situation is evaluated depends in part, at least, on the relevant underlying beliefs. These beliefs are embedded in more or less stable structures, labeled "schemas," that select and synthesize incoming data." Beck, A.T., Freeman, A., Davis, D.D., & Associates (2004). Cognitive therapy of personality disorders. (2nd edition). New York: Guilford, p. 17

Additional sessions can be added if needed. Six to eight targeted assessment sessions are typically sufficient to document the presence or absence of the diagnostic indicators of pathogenic parenting responsible for creating the child's attachment-related pathology surrounding divorce.

Stimulus Control & Behavior Chain Assessment

Authentic parent-child conflict caused by the problematic parenting of the targeted-rejected parent is reflected in a variety of symptom features. One of the clearest indicators of authentic parent-child conflict is through the "stimulus control" exercised on the child's behavior by the parenting behavior of the targeted parent. The construct of "stimulus control" for behavior is an established construct in behavioral psychology and is best explained by analogy to driving behavior and traffic lights.

Driving behavior is under the *stimulus control* of traffic lights. When the light (the stimulus) is green, we go. When the traffic light is red, we stop. Our driving behavior is being ***controlled*** by the ***stimulus*** of the traffic light.

Assessing Stimulus Control:

- In authentic parent-child conflict, the child's behavior is under the *stimulus control* of the parent's behavior.

- If the parent's behavior (the stimulus; the traffic light in the analogy) changes, then there should be a corresponding change in the child's behavior (the driving behavior in the analogy).

- If, however, the child's behavior remains unaffected by changes in the stimulus provided by the parent's behavior, then the child's behavior is NOT under the *stimulus control* of the parent's behavior.

- Interpersonal conflict that is not under the *stimulus control* of the other person's behavior is not authentic to that relationship.

Behavior-Chain Assessment:

The assessment of the *behavior-c*hain sequences surrounding parent-child conflict will reveal the authentic or inauthentic stimulus control for behavior. The behavior chain sequence begins by identifying the specific interaction event that preceded the conflict (called the "cue" that triggered the conflict), followed by the sequence of communication and behavioral responses from each person to the triggering cue, and to each ensuing response that is elicited in subsequent phases of the cuing-behavior conflict sequence. The behavior-chain assessment of parent-child conflict identifies the triggering antecedent for each interactions sequence in the parent-child conflict and establishes the stimulus control linkage between the parent's behavior and the child's behavior.

If the child's conflict with the targeted parent is not being cued (elicited) by the behavior of the targeted parent, then the child's behavior is not under the *stimulus control* of the parent's behavior and is therefore not authentic to that relationship. The inauthenticity of the stimulus control for the child's conflict behavior with the targeted parent would then support the alternative hypothesis that the child's conflict with the targeted parent is being cued by (is under the stimulus control of) the child's cross-generational coalition with the allied and supposedly "favored parent," as described within the family systems literature (Goldenberg & Goldenberg, 2013; Haley, 1977; Minuchin, 1974).

Treatment-Focused Assessment Reports

A treatment-focused assessment represents a structured assessment protocol designed to identify the source of pathogenic parenting surrounding the child's attachment-related symptom display. Documentation of the pathogenic parenting data for the targeted-rejected parent is through the *Parenting Practices Rating Scale*. Documentation of the pathogenic parenting data for the allied parent is through the *Diagnostic Checklist for Pathogenic Parenting*. Based on the data documented by the *Parenting Practices Rating Scale* and the *Diagnostic Checklist for Pathogenic Parenting*, a targeted treatment-focused assessment report (Sample Reports; Appendix 3) can be provided to the Court that identifies the causal source for the pathogenic parenting creating the child's attachment-related pathology based on the data from the *Parenting Practices Rating Scale* and the *Diagnostic Checklist for Pathogenic Parenting*.

The treatment-focused assessment report begins by identifying the scope of the assessment and lists each assessment session with the family members. The report then provides a narrative description of the data documented by the *Parenting Practices Rating Scale* and the *Diagnostic Checklist for Pathogenic Parenting*. The report concludes with treatment-related recommendations for resolving the identified and documented cause of the child's attachment-related pathology, based on the clinical evidence documented by the *Parenting Practices Rating Scale* and the *Diagnostic Checklist for Pathogenic Parenting*. If child abuse concerns emerge from the pathogenic parenting of either parent, then these child abuse concerns are noted in the report and recommendations for treatment are provided.

The completed *Parenting Practices Rating Scale* and the completed *Diagnostic Checklist for Pathogenic Parenting* would be included as appendices to the treatment-focused assessment report. The Court then has available a documented assessment of the causal origins for the child's attachment-related pathology surrounding divorce, recommendations for the treatment resolution of the child's attachment-related pathology, and the data on which the causal origins were identified and the treatment-related recommendations were made.

Appendix 1: Parenting Practices Rating Scale

Parenting Practices Rating Scale

C.A Childress, Psy.D. (2016)

Name of Parent: _____ Date: _____

Indicate all that apply. Do <u>not</u> indicate child abuse is present unless allegations have been confirmed. In cases of abuse allegations that have neither been confirmed nor disconfirmed, or that are unfounded, use Allegation subheading rating <u>not</u> Category rating.

Level 1: Child Abuse

☐ 1. **Sexual Abuse**
As defined by legal statute.
    ☐ Allegation: Neither confirmed nor disconfirmed
    ☐ Allegation: Unfounded

☐ 2. **Physical Abuse**
Hitting the child with a closed fist; striking the child with an open hand or a closed fist around the head or shoulders; striking the child with sufficient force to leave bruises; striking the child with any instrument (weapon) such as kitchen utensils, paddles, straps, belts, or cords.
    ☐ Allegation: Neither confirmed nor disconfirmed
    ☐ Allegation: Unfounded

☐ 3. **Emotional Abuse**
Frequent verbal degradation of the child as a person in a hostile and demeaning tone; frequent humiliation of the child.
    ☐ Allegation: Neither confirmed nor disconfirmed
    ☐ Allegation: Unfounded

☐ 4. **Psychological Abuse**
Pathogenic parenting that creates significant psychological or developmental pathology in the child in order to meet the emotional and psychological needs of the parent, including a role-reversal use of the child as a regulatory object for the parent's emotional and psychological needs.
    ☐ Allegation: Neither confirmed nor disconfirmed
    ☐ Allegation: Unfounded

☐ 5. **Neglect**
Failure to provide for the child's basic needs for food, shelter, safety, and general care.
    ☐ Allegation: Neither confirmed nor disconfirmed
    ☐ Allegation: Unfounded

☐ 6. **Domestic Violence Exposure**
Repeated traumatic exposure of the child to one parent's violent physical assaults toward the other parent or to the repeated emotional degradation (emotional abuse) of the other parent.
    ☐ Allegation: Neither confirmed nor disconfirmed
    ☐ Allegation: Unfounded

Level 2: Severely Problematic Parenting

☐ 7. **Overly Strict Discipline**
Parental discipline practices that are excessively harsh and over-controlling, such as inflicting severe physical discomfort on the child through the use of stress postures, using shaming techniques, or confining the child in an enclosed area for excessively long periods (room time-outs are not overly strict discipline).

☐ 8. **Overly Hostile Parenting**
Frequent displays (more days than not) of excessive parental anger (6 or above on a 10-point scale).

☐ 9. **Overly Disengaged Parenting**
Repeated failure to provide parental supervision and/or age-appropriate limits on the child's behavior and activities; parental major depression or substance abuse problems.

☐ 10. **Overly Involved-Intrusive Parenting**
Enmeshed, over-intrusive, and/or over-anxious parenting that violates the psychological self-integrity of the child; role-reversal use of the child as a regulatory object for the parent's anxiety or narcissistic needs.

☐ 11. **Family Context of High Inter-Spousal Conflict**
Repeated exposure of the child to high inter-spousal conflict that includes excessive displays of inter-spousal anger.

Level 3: Problematic Parenting

☐ 12. **Harsh Discipline**
Excessive use of strict discipline practices in the context of limited displays of parental affection; limited use of parental praise, encouragement, and expressions of appreciation.

☐ 13. **High-Anger Parenting**
Chronic parental irritability and anger and minimal expressions of parental affection.

☐ 14. **Uninvolved Parenting**
Disinterested lack of involvement with the child; emotionally disengaged parenting; parental depression.

☐ 15. **Anxious or Over-Involved Parenting**
Intrusive parenting that does not respect interpersonal boundaries.

☐ 16. **Overwhelmed Parenting**
The parent is overwhelmed by the degree of child emotional-behavioral problems and cannot develop an effective response to the child's emotional-behavioral issues.

☐ 17. **Family Context of Elevated Inter-Spousal Conflict**
Chronic child exposure to moderate-level inter-spousal conflict and anger or intermittent explosive episodes of highly angry inter-spousal conflict (intermittent spousal conflicts involving moderate anger that are successfully resolved are normal-range and are not elevated inter-spousal conflict).

Level 4: Positive Parenting

☐ 18. **Affectionate Involvement – Structured Spectrum**
Parenting includes frequent displays of parental affection and *clearly structured* rules and expectations for the child's behavior. Appropriate discipline follows from clearly defined and appropriate rules.

☐ 19. **Affectionate Involvement – Dialogue Spectrum**
Parenting includes frequent displays of parental affection and *flexibly negotiated* rules and expectations for the child's behavior. Parenting emphasizes dialogue, negotiation, and flexibility.

☐ 20. **Affectionate Involvement – Balanced**
Parenting includes frequent displays of parental affection and parenting effectively balances structured discipline with flexible parent-child dialogue.

Permissive to Authoritarian Dimension Rating: _____

```
|----|----|----|----|----|----|----|----|----|----|
0    10   20   30   40   50   60   70   80   90   100
Permissive            Flexible Dialogue    Structured Discipline    Authoritarian
Parenting             Spectrum             Spectrum                 Parenting
```

Abusive Neglect:		Hostile Abuse:
Extremely disengaged	Balanced Parenting	Extremely hostile
and neglectful parenting		abusive parenting

← Normal Range Parenting →

Capacity for Authentic Empathy Rating:

```
|--------|--------|--------|--------|
1        2        3        4        5
```

1	2	3	4	5
Rigidly self-absorbed perspective; unable to de-center; absence of empathy	Tends to be rigidly self-absorbed; difficulty in de-centering and taking the perspective of others	Self-reflective; able to de-center from personal perspective to take the perspectives of others	Tends to be over-involved; diffusion of psychological boundaries between self-experience and child's experience	Enmeshed loss of psychological boundaries; projective identification of self-experience onto the child
Narcissistic Spectrum		Developmentally Healthy Range Empathy		Borderline Spectrum

Parental Issues of Clinical Concern (CC)

☐ **CC 1:** Parental schizophrenia spectrum issues
    Stabilized on medication?   ☐ Yes   ☐ No   ☐ Variable

☐ **CC 2:** Parental bipolar spectrum issues
    Stabilized on medication?   ☐ Yes   ☐ No   ☐ Variable

☐ **CC 3:** Parental major depression spectrum issues (including suicidality)
    Stabilized by treatment?   ☐ Yes   ☐ No   ☐ Variable

☐ **CC 4:** Parental substance abuse issues
    Treated and in remission (1 yr)?   ☐ Yes   ☐ No   ☐ Variable

☐ **CC 5:** Parental narcissistic or borderline personality disorder traits
    In treatment?   ☐ Yes   ☐ No   ☐ Variable

☐ **CC 6:** Parental history of trauma
    Treated or in treatment?   ☐ Yes   ☐ No   ☐ Variable

Appendix 2: Diagnostic Checklist for Pathogenic Parenting

Diagnostic Checklist for Pathogenic Parenting: Extended Version
C.A. Childress, Psy.D. (2015/2017)

All three of the diagnostic indicators must be present (either 2a OR 2b) for a clinical diagnosis of attachment-based "parental alienation." Sub-threshold clinical presentations can be further evaluated using a "Response to Intervention" trial.

1. Attachment System Suppression

Present	Sub-Threshold	Absent	
☐	☐	☐	The child's symptoms evidence a selective and targeted suppression of the normal-range functioning of the child's attachment bonding motivations toward one parent, the targeted-rejected parent, in which the child seeks to entirely terminate a relationship with this parent (i.e., a child-initiated cutoff in the child's relationship with a normal-range and affectionally available parent).

Secondary Criterion: **Normal-Range Parenting:**

yes	no	
☐	☐	The parenting practices of the targeted-rejected parent are assessed to be broadly normal-range, with due consideration given to the wide spectrum of acceptable parenting that is typically displayed in normal-range families.

Normal-range parenting includes the legitimate exercise of parental prerogatives in establishing desired family values through parental expectations for desired child behavior and normal-range discipline practices.

2(a). Personality Disorder Traits

Present	Sub-Threshold	Absent	
☐	☐	☐	The child's symptoms evidence all five of the following narcissistic/(borderline) personality disorder features displayed toward the targeted-rejected parent.

Sub-Criterion Met

yes	no	
☐	☐	**Grandiosity:** The child displays a grandiose perception of occupying an inappropriately elevated status in the family hierarchy that is above the targeted-rejected parent from which the child feels empowered to sit in judgment of the targeted-rejected parent as both a parent and as a person.
☐	☐	**Absence of Empathy:** The child displays a complete absence of empathy for the emotional pain being inflicted on the targeted-rejected parent by the child's hostility and rejection of this parent.
☐	☐	**Entitlement:** The child displays an over-empowered sense of entitlement in which the child expects that his or her desires will be met by the targeted-rejected parent to the child's satisfaction, and if the rejected parent fails to meet the child's entitled expectations to the child's satisfaction then the child feels entitled to enact a retaliatory punishment on the rejected parent for the child's judgment of parental failures
☐	☐	**Haughty and Arrogant Attitude:** The child displays an attitude of haughty arrogance and contemptuous disdain for the targeted-rejected parent.
☐	☐	**Splitting:** The child evidences polarized extremes of attitude toward the parents, in which the supposedly "favored" parent is idealized as the all-good and nurturing parent while the rejected parent is entirely devalued as the all-bad and entirely inadequate parent.

2(b). Phobic Anxiety Toward a Parent

Present	Sub-Threshold	Absent	
☐	☐	☐	The child's symptoms evidence an extreme and excessive anxiety toward the targeted-rejected parent that meets the following DSM-5 diagnostic criteria for a specific phobia:

Criterion Met

yes	no	
☐	☐	**Persistent Unwarranted Fear**: The child displays a persistent and unwarranted fear of the targeted-rejected parent that is cued either by the presence of the targeted parent or in anticipation of being in the presence of the targeted parent
☐	☐	**Severe Anxiety Response**: The presence of the targeted-rejected parent almost invariably provokes an anxiety response which can reach the levels of a situationally provoked panic attack.
☐	☐	**Avoidance of Parent**: The child seeks to avoid exposure to the targeted parent due to the situationally provoked anxiety or else endures the presence of the targeted parent with great distress.

3. Fixed False Belief

Present	Sub-Threshold	Absent	
☐	☐	☐	The child's symptoms display an intransigently held, fixed and false belief maintained despite contrary evidence (a delusion) regarding the child's supposed "victimization" by the normal-range parenting of the targeted-rejected parent (an encapsulated persecutory delusion). The child's beliefs carry the implication that the normal-range parenting of the targeted-rejected parent are somehow "abusive" toward the child. The parenting practices of the targeted-rejected parent are assessed to be broadly normal-range.

DSM-5 Diagnosis

If the three diagnostic indicators of attachment-based "parental alienation" are present in the child's symptom display (either 2a or 2b), the appropriate DSM-5 diagnosis is:

<u>DSM-5 Diagnosis</u>

    309.4 Adjustment Disorder with mixed disturbance of emotions and conduct

    V61.20 Parent-Child Relational Problem

    V61.29 Child Affected by Parental Relationship Distress

    V995.51 Child Psychological Abuse, Confirmed (pathogenic parenting)

Checklist of Associated Clinical Signs (ACS)

evident	not evident	
☐	☐	ACS 1: Use of the Word "Forced"
☐	☐	ACS 2: Enhancing Child Empowerment to Reject the Other Parent

evident	not evident	
☐	☐	"Child should decide on visitation"
☐	☐	"Listen to the child"
☐	☐	Advocating for child testimony

evident	not evident	
☐	☐	ACS 3: The Exclusion Demand
☐	☐	ACS 4: Parental Replacement
☐	☐	ACS 5: The Unforgivable Event
☐	☐	ACS 6: Liar – Fake
☐	☐	ACS 7: Themes for Rejection

evident	not evident	
☐	☐	Too Controlling
☐	☐	Anger management
☐	☐	Targeted parent doesn't take responsibility/apologize
☐	☐	New romantic relationship neglects the child
☐	☐	Prior neglect of the child by the parent
☐	☐	Vague personhood of the targeted parent
☐	☐	Non-forgivable grudge
☐	☐	Not feeding the child

evident	not evident	
☐	☐	ACS 8: Unwarranted Use of the Word "Abuse"
☐	☐	ACS 9: Excessive Texting, Phone Calls, and Emails
☐	☐	ACS 10: Role-Reversal Use of the Child ("It's not me, it's the child who…")
☐	☐	ACS 11: Targeted Parent "Deserves to be Rejected"
☐	☐	ACS 12: Allied Parent Disregards Court Orders and Court Authority

evident	not evident	
☐	☐	Child disregard of court orders for custody
☐	☐	Child runaway behavior from the targeted parent

Appendix 3: Sample Treatment-Focused Assessment Reports

A Treatment-Focused Assessment Report Example for a Confirmed Diagnosis of Pathogenic Parenting

Date: <Date of Assessment>
Psychologist: <Psychologist's Name>

Scope of Report

A Treatment-Focused Assessment was requested by the Court for the parent-child relationship of John Doe (DOB: 1/15/08) with his mother regarding their estranged and conflictual relationship. This treatment-focused assessment report is based on the following family interviews:

<date>: Clinical interview with mother
<date>: Clinical interview with father
<date>: Clinical interview with child
<date>: Clinical relationship assessment with mother and child
<date>: Clinical interview with mother
<date>: Clinical relationship assessment with mother and child
<date>: Clinical interview with father

Rating Scales Completed (appended)

Parenting Practices Rating Scale (mother)
Diagnostic Checklist for Pathogenic Parenting

Results of Assessment

Based on the clinical assessments, the child displays the three symptom indicators of pathogenic parenting associated with an attachment-based model of "parental alienation" (AB-PA; Childress, 2015):

1) **Attachment System Suppression:** A targeted and selective suppression of the child's attachment bonding motivations relative to his mother in the absence of sufficiently distorted parenting practices from the mother that would account for the suppression of the child's attachment system;

2) **Personality Disorder Traits:** A set of five specific narcissistic/borderline personality disorder features are present in the child's symptom display;

3) **Encapsulated Delusional Belief System:** The child evidences an intransigently held fixed and false belief that is maintained despite contrary evidence (i.e., an encapsulated delusion) regarding the child's supposed "victimization" by the normal-range parenting of the mother (i.e., an encapsulated persecutory delusion).

The presence of this specific symptom pattern in a child's symptom display is consistent with an attachment-based framework for conceptualizing "parental alienation" processes within the family that involve an induced suppression of the child's attachment bonding motivations toward a normal-range and affectionally available parent (i.e., the targeted parent) as a result of the distorted parenting practices of a personality disordered parent (i.e., narcissistic/borderline features, which accounts for the presence of these features in the child's symptom display).

The mother's parenting practices on the *Parenting Practices Rating Scale* are assessed to be broadly normal-range. The mother's parenting would be classified as Level 4, Positive Parenting; Affectionate Involvement – Structured Spectrum. The mother establishes clearly defined rules and expectations for child behavior that are well within normal-range parenting, and the mother's delivery of consequences is fair and is based on these established rules and expectations for child behavior. The mother offers parental encouragement and affection, but these offers of parental affection are typically rejected by the child. The mother's rating on the Permissive to Authoritarian Dimension would be 60, which is well within normal-range parenting. She tends toward the use of clearly established rules and appropriate parental discipline for child non-compliance. The mother's capacity for authentic empathy is normal-range. She is able to self-reflect on her actions and also de-center from her own perspective to adopt the frame of reference of other people. She is not overly self-involved nor does she project her own emotional needs into and onto the child. There are no issues of clinical concern regarding the mother's parenting.

DSM-5 Diagnosis

The combined presence in the child's symptom display of significant attachment-related developmental pathology (diagnostic indicator 1), narcissistic personality disorder pathology (diagnostic indicator 2), and delusional-psychiatric pathology (diagnostic indicator 3) represents definitive diagnostic evidence of pathogenic parenting by an allied parent with prominent narcissistic and/or borderline personality traits, since no other pathology will account for this specific symptom pattern other than pathogenic parenting by an allied narcissistic/borderline personality parent. This set of severe child symptoms warrants the following DSM-5 diagnosis for the child:

309.4 Adjustment Disorder with mixed disturbance of emotions and conduct

V61.20 Parent-Child Relational Problem

V61.29 Child Affected by Parental Relationship Distress

V995.51 Child Psychological Abuse, Confirmed (pathogenic parenting)

Treatment Indications

A confirmed DSM-5 diagnosis of Child Psychological Abuse warrants the following child protection and treatment response:

1.) **Protective Separation Period:** A period of protective separation of the child from the psychologically abusive parenting practices of the allied parent is required in order to protect the child from ongoing exposure to psychologically abusive parenting practices and allow for the treatment and recovery of the child's normal-range and healthy development. Attempting therapy without first establishing a period of protective separation from the pathogenic parenting practices of the father will continue the child's ongoing exposure to the psychologically abusive parenting of the father that is creating significant developmental pathology, personality disorder pathology, and delusional-psychiatric pathology in the child, and will lead to the child becoming a "psychological battleground" between the treatment goals of restoring the child's healthy and normal-range development and the continuing pathogenic goals of the father to create and maintain the child's pathology.

2.) **Treatment:** Appropriate parent-child psychotherapy should be initiated to recover and heal the damaged parent-child affectional bond with the mother and resolve the impact of the prior psychological abuse inflicted on the child by the father's distorted and psychologically abusive parenting practices in order to restore the child's healthy emotional and psychological development.

3.) **Collateral Therapy:** The father should be required to obtain collateral individual therapy with the treatment goal of fostering insight into the cause of the prior abusive parenting practices.

4.) **End of Protective Separation:** The protective separation period should be ended once the child's symptoms associated with the prior psychologically abusive parenting practices of the father are successfully resolved and the child's recovery is stabilized.

5.) **Restoration of the Relationship with the Abusive Parent:** The restoration of the child's relationship with the formerly abusive parent should include sufficient safeguards to ensure that the psychological abuse of the child does not resume once contact with the father is restored. The demonstrated cooperation of the father with his individual collateral therapy and his demonstrated insight into the cause of the prior psychological abuse of the child would represent important considerations in the level of safeguards needed to ensure the child's protection.

6.) **Relapse:** If the child's symptoms reoccur once the child's contact with the father is restored, then another period of protective separation will be needed in order to again recover the child's normal-range and healthy development, and additional protective safeguards will be warranted prior to once again exposing the child to the pathogenic parenting practices of the father.

<u>Child Response to a Protective Separation</u>

The child may initially respond to a protective separation from the currently allied parent (i.e., the father) with increased protest behavior and defiance. This child response represents an emotional-behavioral tantrum reflecting the child's currently over-empowered status relative to accepting authority (i.e. both parental authority and the authority of the Court). Responding to emotional displays of child tantrum behaviors with calm and steady purpose that restores the child to an appropriate social and family hierarchy of cooperation with Court and parental authority will be important to supporting successful family therapy and the resolution of the child's symptoms. Any concern regarding the child's expressed distress at the protective separation from the currently allied parent (i.e., the father) should recognize that the child is fully capable of ending the protective separation period by becoming non-symptomatic. If the child wishes a termination of the protective separation period, then the child simply needs to evidence normal-range affectional child behavior in response to the normal-range parenting practices of the mother, which is under the treatment-related monitoring of the family therapist.

<u>Ending the Protective Separation Period</u>

The protective separation period from the pathogenic and psychologically abusive parenting practices of the allied parent should be ended upon the successful treatment and resolution of the child's symptoms and restoration of the child's healthy and normal-range development. The treating family therapist should seek Court approval to end the child's protective separation from the pathogenic parenting practices of the currently allied parent (i.e., the father) based on the treatment-related gains achieved. Progress reports to the parents and to the Court from the treating family therapist should be provided at least every six months.

A Treatment-Focused Assessment Report Example for
Sub-Threshold Symptoms for the Diagnosis of Pathogenic Parenting

Date: <Date>
Psychologist: <Psychologist's Name>

Scope of Report

A treatment-focused assessment was requested by the Court for the parent-child relationship of John Doe (DOB: 1/15/08) with his mother regarding their estranged and conflictual relationship. This treatment-focused assessment report is based on the following family interviews:

<date>: Clinical interview with mother
<date>: Clinical interview with father
<date>: Clinical interview with child
<date>: Clinical relationship assessment with mother and child
<date>: Clinical interview with mother
<date>: Clinical relationship assessment with mother and child
<date>: Clinical interview with father

Rating Scales Completed (appended)

Parenting Practices Rating Scale (mother)
Diagnostic Checklist for Pathogenic Parenting

Results of Assessment

Based on the clinical assessments, the child does not display the three symptom indicators of pathogenic parenting associated with an attachment-based model of "parental alienation" (AB-PA; Childress, 2015):

1) **Attachment System Suppression:** A targeted and selective suppression of the child's attachment bonding motivations relative to his mother in the absence of sufficiently distorted parenting practices from the mother that would account for the suppression of the child's attachment system;

2) **Personality Disorder Traits:** A set of five specific narcissistic/borderline personality disorder features are present in the child's symptom display;

3) **Encapsulated Delusional Belief System:** The child evidences an intransigently held fixed and false belief that is maintained despite contrary evidence (i.e., an encapsulated delusion) regarding the child's supposed "victimization" by the normal-range parenting of the mother (i.e., an encapsulated persecutory delusion).

The child's symptom presentation does not fully evidence an intransigently held fixed-and-false belief in the child's supposed "victimization" because the mother's parenting practices are sufficiently problematic to warrant concerns that the child's perceptions of his mother have some component of accuracy. In addition, John expressed an openness to restoring a relationship with his mother if his potentially reality-based concerns can be adequately addressed.

However, John also evidenced a prominent suppression of normal-range attachment bonding motivation toward his mother and he displayed prominent signs of narcissistic personality disorder features in his attitude and responses to his mother. The symptom features in the family also evidenced several Associated Clinical Signs (see attached *Diagnostic Checklist for Pathogenic Parenting*), so that concerns regarding the potential pathogenic influence of the currently allied and supposedly "favored" parent (i.e., the father) continue.

Mother's Parenting Practices

The mother's parenting practices are assessed to be in the Level 3 domain on the *Parenting Practices Rating Scale* (Problematic Parenting), reflecting potentially harsh discipline (Item 12) and high-anger parenting (Item 13). These parenting practices, however, may also be a product of the child's provoking these parenting responses through a high level of child non-compliance and disrespect for parental authority. A Response-to-Intervention (RTI) assessment would help clarify the causal direction for the parent-child conflict.

The child is also likely impacted by chronic exposure to high levels of inter-spousal conflict involving intermittent explosive anger from one spouse directed toward the other spouse (Item 16). While this inter-spousal anger is not directed toward the child, the extent of the high inter-spousal conflict likely creates considerable stress for the child and represents a degree of parental insensitivity for the child's emotional and psychological needs by at least one, and possibly both, parents. Restricting the expression of inter-spousal anger and developing cooperative co-parenting spousal skills of respecting boundaries and for mutual displays of kindness in respectful communication would be in the emotional and psychological best interests of the child.

The mother appears to employ a more disciplinarian approach to parenting involving structured rules and consequences, and her rating on the Permissive to Authoritarian Dimension would be in the 60 to 70 range, which is in the normal-range of parenting. A reduction in parent-child conflict might be achieved by helping the mother expand her parenting options by using increased dialogue and negotiation skills that would shift her rating on the Permissive to Authoritarian Dimension into the mid-range of 45 to 55. However, it should also be noted that the mother's current parenting practices are well within the normal-range for parenting generally, and considerable latitude should be granted to parents to establish rules and values within their families that are consistent with their cultural and personal value systems.

The mother's capacity for authentic empathy with the child appears to be in the normal range. She is able to self-reflect on her own behavior and she is also able to de-center from her own perspective to view situations from alternate points of view. The mother does not appear to become overly self-involved in needing to have her perspective validated, nor does she appear to project her own needs onto the child.

There are no areas of clinical concern related to the mother's parenting.

Treatment Indications

Based on the set of symptom features in child's symptom display and the assessment of the mother's current parenting practices, a Response-to-Intervention (RTI) treatment approach is recommended for a 6-month period to further assess the role of the mother's parenting practices relative to the potential role of pathogenic parental influence from the father in creating and supporting the child's symptomatic relationship with his mother.

1.) Response to Intervention (RTI) Assessment

A 6-month period of family therapy is recommended that includes both mother-child therapy sessions to improve communication and conflict resolution skills as well as collateral sessions with the mother to expand and improve her parenting responses to John.

Authentic Parent-Child Conflict-Resolution: If the mother displays normal-range and appropriate parenting in response to treatment directives, then John's behavior toward his mother should show corresponding improvement (i.e., demonstrating that the child's behavior is under the "stimulus control" of the parent's behavior, meaning that the parent-child conflict is authentic to their relationship features). Changes to the mother's parenting practices will then lead to a resolution of the parent-child conflict.

Authentic Parent-Child Conflict–No Resolution: If the mother is unable to sufficiently alter her potentially harsh discipline and high-anger parenting behavior in response to treatment directives, then this would represent suggestive clinical evidence that the source of the mother-son conflict is potentially authentic to their relationship dynamics, and family therapy should continue to seek changes in the mother's parenting responses toward a more nurturing and affectionate parenting approach to help resolve the parent-child conflict.

Inauthentic Parent-Child Conflict: If, however, the mother displays normal-range and appropriate parenting in response to treatment directives, and John's symptoms continue despite changes in the mother's parenting practices, then this would represent confirming diagnostic evidence that John's behavior is <u>not</u> under the "stimulus control" of his mother's behavior and her responses to him, meaning that he is <u>not</u> responding to authentic difficulties in the mother-son relationship. The continuance of John's symptomatic behavior toward his mother despite changes in the mother's parenting practices would represent diagnostic evidence that John's symptomatic responses to his mother are likely being created by the pathogenic parenting practices of the father (through the formation of a cross-generational coalition of the child with his father against the mother). A treatment plan to address the pathogenic parenting of the father in creating the child's ongoing conflict with the mother should then be developed and implemented (and a period of protective separation from the father's pathogenic parenting may be warranted).

2.) Compliance with Court Orders for Custody and Visitation

All parties, including the child, should comply fully with all Court orders including those for custody and visitation. Failure by the currently allied and supposedly "favored" parent (i.e., the father) to comply with Court orders for custody and visitation should be viewed as non-compliance with treatment, and a follow-up treatment-focused assessment should be initiated (at the written recommendation of the treating family therapist) to determine whether a protective separation of the child from the potentially pathogenic parenting practices of the father is needed to allow for effective treatment.

Child noncompliance with Court orders for custody and visitation, such as refusing custody time-share visitations with the mother, should be ascribed as a serious failure in parenting by the currently allied and supposedly "favored" parent (i.e., the father) representing a parental failure to demonstrate appropriate parental responsibility.

- If the father is instructing the child to comply with the father's directive to cooperate with the mother's custody and visitation time and the child is refusing to comply with the father's directive, then the child is evidencing oppositional non-compliant behavior relative to the father's parental authority and the authority of the Court.
- As the allied and supposedly "favored" parent, the child's behavior is a reflection of the parenting received from the father, so that the child's oppositional non-compliance with the father's parental authority and the authority of the Court is a direct reflection on the father's parenting and his capacity for providing appropriate parental guidance to the child.

A failure to exercise effective parental responsibility and guidance by the allied and supposedly "favored" parent should be viewed as representing the father's non-compliance with the requirements of treatment by failing to exercise appropriate parental responsibility and child guidance as the "favored" and allied parent. The child's refusal to comply with Court orders, including all orders for custody and visitation, and the child's direct defiance of the father's parental authority should trigger a follow-up treatment-focused assessment (at the written recommendation of the treating family therapist) to determine whether a change in the responsible parent is needed to allow for effective treatment and the recovery of the child's normal-range and healthy development.

In any follow-up treatment-focused assessment, primary consideration should be afforded to the treatment needs of the child in establishing the treatment-related conditions necessary for effective treatment. The treatment-related needs of the child should be given precedence over parental considerations of being "favored" or "unfavored" by the child. If the allied and supposedly "favored" parent cannot establish the conditions necessary for the effective resolution of the child's symptoms, then a change in the responsible parent may be necessary due to the then demonstrated parental failure of the allied and supposedly "favored" parent to enact the appropriate parental authority and guidance necessary for the child's successful treatment.

Progress reports to the parents and to the Court from the treating family therapist should be provided at least every six months.

Made in the USA
Lexington, KY
28 April 2019